Quick Reference Scripture Handbook

by
Dick Mills

HARRISON HOUSE
Tulsa, Oklahoma

Unless otherwise indicated, all
Scripture quotations are taken from
the *King James Version* of the Bible.

5th Printing
Over 35,000 in Print

Quick Reference Scripture Handbook
ISBN 0-89274-323-9
Copyright © 1984 by Dick Mills
P. O. Box 758
Hemet, California 92343

Published by Harrison House, Inc.
P. O. Box 35035
Tulsa, Oklahoma 74153

Printed in the United States of America.
All rights reserved under International
Copyright Law. Contents and/or cover may
not be reproduced in whole or in part in any
form without the express written consent
of the publisher.

A

ABIDING in the Lord
Ps. 91:1
John 15:5,7

ABUNDANCE (*See also* Blessings, Faithfulness)

Abundance of BLESSINGS promised believers
John 10:10
2 Cor. 9:8
Eph. 3:20,21

FAITH AND LOVE 1 Tim. 1:14
FRUITFULNESS Ex. 1:7; Is. 35:1,2
GOODNESS Ex. 34:6
GRACE Rom. 5:17; 2 Cor. 4:15
JOY Ps. 36:8; 2 Cor. 8:1,2
MERCY 1 Pet. 1:3
PARDON Is. 55:7
PEACE Jer. 33:6; Ps. 37:11
                            72:1,7
PROVISION 1 Chron. 22:5
                 Ps. 132:13,15
RAIN 1 Kings 18:41; Ps. 65:10
SATISFACTION Ps. 36:8
UTTERANCE OF PRAISE Ps. 145:7

ACTING wisely
1 Sam. 18:14
Ps. 101:2
Prov. 16:20
     28:26

ACTION—being stirred up
Ex. 35:21
Ezra 1:1
Hag. 1:14

A

AGREEMENT of heart and mouth

Ps. 19:14
  116:10
Prov. 16:23
Rom. 10:8

ANOINTED

By the HOLY SPIRIT for service
(*See also* Serving the Lord)

1 Sam. 16:13
Acts 10:38

By the LORD

Ps. 23:5
  45:7
  89:20
  92:10
Is. 61:1
2 Cor. 1:21

ANSWERS—immediate answers from God

Mark 1:31
  2:11,12
John 6:19-21
Acts 3:7
  9:34

APPEARANCE of Christ at His Second Coming

Col. 3:4
Titus 2:11-13
1 John 3:2

APPETITE—spiritual appetite and thirst

Ps. 63:1
  107:9
Matt. 5:6

ASSURANCE promised

>Is. 32:17
>Acts 17:29-31
>1 Thess. 1:5
>Heb. 10:22

ATTITUDE—keeping a right attitude

>Lev. 19:18
>Prov. 4:23
>Matt. 15:18-20

ATTRACTION of Christ

>Gen. 49:10
>Ps. 65:2
>Mark 1:33
> 5:21
> 12:37
>John 12:32

ATTRACTIVENESS of the Christ-centered personality

>Job 11:19
>Ps. 142:7
>Is. 49:23
> 60:3-5

BANNER—having one over us

>Ps. 60:4
>Song of Sol. 2:4
>Is. 13:2

BAPTISM

HOLY SPIRIT baptism promised
>Acts 1:5,8
> 2:38
>John 7:38,39

Needing WATER baptism
>Matt. 28:19

B

Mark 16:16
Col. 2:10-12

BEAUTY of the Lord

Ps. 29:2
    45:11
    90:17
Is. 61:1,3

BELIEVER—standing firm as a believer (*See also* Stand)

Ex. 14:13,14
2 Chron. 20:17
Gal. 5:1
Eph. 6:11-18

BELIEVERS—two are better than one

Deut. 32:30
Eccl. 4:9
Amos 3:3
Matt. 18:19

BITTERNESS—keeping bitterness out of your heart

Prov. 4:23
Eph. 4:31
Heb. 12:15

BLESSING—today is the day of blessing

Ps. 118:24
Hag. 2:19
Matt. 6:11
2 Cor. 6:2

BLOOD OF JESUS
ATONES for us Lev. 17:11
CLEANSES 1 John 1:7
DEFEATS Satan for us Rev. 12:11
JUSTIFIES Rom. 5:8,9
PURCHASES Acts 20:28
PURGES Heb. 9:13,14
REDEEMS Col. 1:12-14
REMITS sins Matt. 26:27,28
WASHES Rev. 1:4,5

BLESSINGS (*See also* Abundance; Faithfulness)
Blessings upon CHILDREN
  Ps. 115:14
  Is. 8:18
    49:25
    54:13
DOUBLE portion
  2 Kings 2:9
  Is. 61:7
  Zech. 9:12
FAR beyond our fondest expectations
  Hab. 1:5
  2 Cor. 9:8
  Eph. 3:20,21
NEW AND OLD
  Lev. 26:10
  Song of Sol. 7:13
  Matt. 13:52
NEW BLESSINGS of salvation
  Ezek. 36:26
  Mark 2:22
  2 Cor. 5:17

B

PROMISED by God (*See also* Promises of God)
- Deut. 28:8
- 2 Sam. 7:29
- Prov. 10:22

SURPLUS
- Prov. 28:20
- Matt. 13:12
- John 10:10
- 2 Cor. 9:8
- Eph. 3:20,21

BODY—general verses for the physical body

- 1 Cor. 6:13,20
- 1 Thess. 5:23

AILMENTS inside the body
- Ex. 23:25
- Deut. 7:15
- Zeph. 3:17

ANKLES

...there was not one feeble person among their tribes (Ps. 105:37).

Note: According to *Strong's Exhaustive Concordance of the Bible*, the Hebrew word for *feeble* is *kashal*. It means "...to totter or waver (through weakness of the legs, espec. the ankle); by impl. to falter, stumble, faint or fall...." None of Israel's marching population was handicapped with weak ankles.

BONES
- Prov. 3:1-8
- 16:24

Is. 58:11
EARS
Prov. 20:12
Is. 32:3
Luke 7:22
EYES
Deut. 34:7
Prov. 20:12
Is. 32:3
FEET
1 Sam. 2:9
Ps. 116:8
Prov. 3:23
HANDS
Eccl. 9:10
Is. 35:3
Heb. 12:12
HEART
Ps. 27:14
    31:24
    73:26
NIGHTMARES
Job 11:18
Prov. 3:24
    6:20-22
PERIODIC DISCOMFORT of women
Ps. 41:3
PRE-NATAL assurances
Is. 40:11
   66:9
1 Tim. 2:15
SKIN
2 Kings 5:14
Job 33:25
Eph. 5:30

B—C

SLEEPLESSNESS (*See also* Sleep)
Ps. 3:5
4:8
127:2

BOLDNESS in the Lord

Prov. 28:1
Acts 4:31
Eph. 3:11,12

CALLING on the Lord

Ps. 50:15
Jer. 33:3
Rom. 10:13

CHILDREN having a relish for God's Word

Deut. 6:6,7
Ps. 119:9,11
2 Tim. 3:15

CHRISTIANITY

LIKENED to a footrace
1 Cor. 9:24
Phil. 3:14
Heb. 12:1
SOUND Christianity
DOCTRINE Titus 2:1-3
FAITH Titus 1:13
HEART Prov. 14:30
MIND 2 Tim. 1:7
SPEECH Titus 2:8
WISDOM Prov. 2:7

CHRISTIANS

Christians LIKENED to fruitful trees
Ps. 1:3

Is. 37:31
    61:1,3
Christians REFRESHING
other Christians
    Rom. 15:30-32
    1 Cor. 16:18
    2 Tim. 1:16

DAY—children of the day

    Rom. 13:13
    John 9:4
    1 Thess. 5:5,7

DEFEAT—apparent defeat turned to victory (*See also* Satan, Victory of Christians; Victory)

    Deut. 28:7
        33:29
    Neh. 13:2
    Esth. 7:10
    Ps. 9:13-15

DEFENSE—The Lord is our defense (*See also* Satan)

    Ps. 7:10
        20:1
        59:17

DELIGHTING in the Lord

    Ps. 37:4,23
        40:8
    Is. 58:14

DELIVERANCE

Deliverance with
ENLARGEMENT
    Esth. 4:13,14

D

Ps. 4:1
  18:36
  66:12
  118:5

Deliverance PROMISED
  Is. 46:4
  2 Cor. 1:9,10

From TROUBLE (*See also* Trusting in the Lord)
  Job 5:19
  Ps. 34:17
    50:15
  Prov. 12:13

DISCERNMENT is needed and available
  Ezek. 44:23
  Mal. 3:18
  1 Cor. 12:7-10

DISCRETION
  Ps. 112:5
  Prov. 1:1,4
    2:11
    3:21
    19:11

DOING God's will
  Ps. 40:8
    143:10
  Eph. 5:17
  1 John 2:17

DOING good
  The LORD doing good
    Jer. 32:41
    Mic. 7:8
    Acts 10:38

The LORD'S SERVANTS doing good
- Ps. 34:14
- Gal. 6:9
- Heb. 13:16
- 3 John 11

DOORS—new open doors
- Is. 45:2,3
- 1 Cor. 16:9
- Rev. 3:7,8

ENCOURAGED by the Lord
- Josh. 1:9
- 1 Sam. 30:6
- Ps. 34:5

ENCOURAGING fellow believers
- Eph. 4:32
- 1 Thess. 4:18
- Heb. 3:13
- James 5:16

ESTABLISHED in life
- Is. 54:14
- Rom 1:11
- 2 Cor. 1:21

EYES of the Lord
- 2 Chron. 16:9
- Ps. 34:15
- Prov. 15:3

EXCHANGE in kind
- 1 Sam 2:30
- Prov. 11:25
- Luke 6:38
- James 4:8

E—F

EXPECTING good things from the Lord

Ps. 9:18
62:5
Prov. 23:18
24:14
Phil. 1:20

FAITH (*See also* Fruit, Faith)

Mark 11:22
Rom. 10:17
12:3
Eph. 2:8,9
Faith OF GOD
Acts 3:16
Gal. 2:16,20

FAITHFULNESS

Ps. 31:23
Prov. 13:17
BRINGS BLESSINGS (*See also* Abundance, Blessings)
Ps. 84:4
Prov. 25:13
28:20

FAMINE—God keeps believers alive during famine

Job 5:19,20
Ps. 33:18,19
37:19
Prov. 10:3

FASTING enjoined

Ps. 35:13
Joel 2:12
Matt. 6:17,18

FAVOR with God and man

1 Sam. 2:26
Prov. 3:4
Luke 2:52

FEET (*See also* Body, Feet)

And the GOSPEL
Is. 52:7
Rom. 16:20
Eph. 6:15

Of the believers PROTECTED
1 Sam. 2:9
2 Sam. 22:34
Ps. 116:8

Of the believer and
SPIRITUAL WARFARE
Luke 10:19
Rom. 16:20
Eph. 6:15

FLESH VS. SPIRIT

Matt. 26:41
Gal. 5:16,17

FORGIVING OTHERS

Matt. 18:35
For HURTING you
Mark 11:25
Eph. 4:32
Col. 3:13

FRAGRANCE—Spiritual fragrance

Prov. 27:9
2 Cor. 2:15
Phil. 4:18
Rev. 5:8

F

FREEDOM from life's chains
Gen. 41:14
Jer. 40:4
Acts 16:26

FRIENDSHIP
Prov. 17:17
18:24
27:17

A GIFT from the Lord
John 15:14

With the LORD
Matt. 11:19
John 15:13-15

FRUITFULNESS—spiritual fruitfulness
Ps. 1:3
John 15:8
Eph. 5:9
Heb. 12:11

FRUIT OF THE SPIRIT
Gal. 5:22,23

FAITH
Eph. 2:8
2 Thess. 1:3
1 Tim. 6:12

GENTLENESS
Ps. 18:35
2 Cor. 10:1
2 Tim. 2:24

GOODNESS
Rom. 15:14
Eph. 5:9
2 Thess. 1:11

JOY
- Acts 13:52
- Rom. 14:17
- 15:13

LONGSUFFERING
- 2 Cor. 6:4-6
- Eph. 4:1,2
- Col. 1:9-11
- 3:12

LOVE
- 1 John 4:8,18
- Jude 21

MEEKNESS
- Col. 3:12
- 1 Tim. 6:11
- Titus 3:1,2

PEACE
- John 14:27
- Rom. 5:1
- Col. 3:15

TEMPERANCE (self-control)
- 1 Cor. 9:25
- Titus 1:7,8
- 2 Pet. 1:5,6

FULLNESS OF GOD

- John 1:16
- Eph. 1:23
- 3:19
- 4:13
- Col. 1:19
- 2:9

GARMENTS—spiritual garments for the believer

- BEAUTY Is. 52:1
- GLADNESS Ps. 30:11

G

GLORY Ps. 45:13
HUMILITY 1 Pet. 5:5
PRAISE Is. 61:1-3
RIGHTEOUSNESS Is. 61:10
SALVATION Ps. 132:16
WEDDING garment Rev. 19:7,8

GIFTS of God for us

Rom. 1:11
1 Cor. 1:4-7
Eph. 4:8

GIFTS OF THE SPIRIT

1 Cor. 1:4-7
    12:8-10,31
Heb. 2:3,4

COVET the gifts
1 Cor. 12:31
    14:1,12

DISCERNING of spirits
1 Kings 3:9
Ezek. 44:23
Mal. 3:18

GIFT OF FAITH
Luke 17:5
1 John 5:4
Jude 20

GIFT OF PROPHECY
Rom. 12:5,6
1 Cor. 13:9
    14:31

GIFTS OF HEALING
Mal. 4:2
Acts 4:22
1 Cor. 12:28

TONGUES—DIVERS kinds of tongues
  1 Cor. 12:28
      14:21,39
TONGUES—INTERPRETATION of tongues
  1 Cor. 14:13,26,27
WORD OF KNOWLEDGE
  Prov. 17:27
      19:27
      23:12
WORD OF WISDOM
  Eccl. 12:11
  1 Cor. 2:6,7,13
WORKING OF MIRACLES
  Acts 15:12
  Gal. 3:5
  Heb. 2:4

God LOOKING for a man

2 Chron. 16:9
Jer. 5:1
Ezek. 22:30

God of the MOUNTAINS AND HILLS

1 Kings 20:23,28
Ps. 72:3
   125:2

God of the VALLEYS

1 Kings 20:23,28
Ps. 84:5,6
Song of Sol. 2:1
Is. 41:18

God SEARCHING OUR HEARTS

1 Chron. 28:9
Ps. 139:23
Jer. 17:10

G

God TOUCHING A CITY
Ps. 144:10-14
Acts 8:8
　　18:9,10

God WORKING QUICKLY
2 Chron. 29:35,36
Is. 60:22
Rom. 9:28

GRANDCHILDREN
Ps. 103:17
　　128:5,6
Prov. 13:22
Is. 44:3
　　59:21

GROWTH—slow and steady
Ex. 23:30
Prov. 4:18
Is. 28:10
Rom. 1:17

GUIDANCE
DIRECTIONS from the Lord
　Ps. 37:23
　Prov. 3:5,6
　　　16:9
By a DREAM
　Job 33:14-16
　Matt. 2:12,19,22
PROMISED by God
　Ps. 32:8
　　　73:24
　Is. 58:11
　Luke 1:76-79
　John 16:13

G—H

SOMETIMES GOD SAYS...
- "Don't be in a hurry."
    - Prov. 19:2
    - Is. 28:16
    - 52:12
- "Go."
    - Gen. 28:15
    - Judg. 6:14
    - Acts 5:20
- "I'm way ahead of you."
    - Is. 65:24
    - Matt. 6:8,32
- "Speed it up."
    - 2 Chron. 24:5
    - Ps. 119:60
    - Is. 51:14
- "Stay."
    - Deut. 10:10
    - 1 Sam. 15:16
    - 30:9
    - Acts 19:22
- "This is it."
    - Ps. 78:65,66
    - Is. 25:9
    - 33:10
- "This isn't it."
    - Gen. 31:13
    - Is. 52:11
    - Mic. 2:10
- "Wait."
    - Ps. 40:1
    - Prov. 20:22
    - Is. 30:18

HAND—the hand of the Lord

Ezra 8:22

H

Ps. 139:5
　　145:16

HANDS

BLESSING OTHERS with them
　Mark 16:18
　Acts 5:12
　　　19:11

GOD BLESSES the works of our hands
　2 Chron. 15:7
　Ps. 90:17
　Is. 65:22

LIFTING UP holy hands to bless the Lord
　Ps. 28:2
　　　63:4
　　　134:2
　　　141:2
　　　143:6
　Lam. 3:41
　1 Tim. 2:8

HEALING

Ps. 30:2
　　103:3
　　147:3
Is. 53:5

HEALTH

Prov. 4:20-22
　　　16:24
Is. 58:8
Jer. 30:17

HOLINESS

Deut. 23:14
Is. 35:8

Ezek. 44:23
2 Cor. 6:17

HOLY SPIRIT

ACTIVE internal energizing of the Holy Spirit

Eph. 3:20,21
Phil. 2:13
Col. 1:29

The NEED to be filled with the Spirit

Acts 11:24
 13:52
Eph. 5:18

HONESTY—a call to honesty

Rom. 12:17
 13:13
1 Thess. 4:10-12
1 Tim. 2:1,2
Heb. 13:18
1 Pet. 2:11,12

HOPE

Job 11:18
Prov. 10:28
Rom. 5:5
Col. 1:25-27
1 John 3:2,3

IMMUNITY

BELIEVERS' IMMUNITY from OCCULT OPPOSITION

Num. 23:23
Neh. 13:1,2
Prov. 26:2

I—J

From CRITICISM
> Job 5:21
> Ps. 31:20
> Is. 54:17

INCREASE given by God
> Ps. 115:14
> Luke 17:5
> 1 Cor. 3:6

INTERCESSORS—the need for intercessors
> Jer. 9:17,18
> Lam. 2:19
> Joel 2:17
> Rom. 8:26

JOY

FOLLOWS STRESS AND PRESSURE
> Ps. 30:5
>   90:15
>   126:5

In BEING SPIRIT FILLED
> Acts 13:52
> Rom. 14:17
> Gal. 5:22

In EXPERIENCING GOD'S MIRACULOUS POWER
> Ps. 126:1,2
> Acts 8:6-8
> 1 Pet. 4:14

In GOING TO CHURCH
> Ps. 84:4
>   100:4
>   122:1

J—K

In READING THE BIBLE
- Ps. 119:162,171
- Jer. 15:16

In the LIFE OF PRAYER
- John 16:24
- Phil. 4:4-6
- 1 John 3:22

In SALVATION
- Ps. 132:16
- Is. 12:3
- Acts 15:3

REPLACING SORROW
- Ps. 30:5,11
- 126:5
- Luke 6:21

JUDGE, humble, chasten yourself

- Ps. 35:13
- 69:10
- 1 Cor. 11:31

KNOWLEDGE

FULL knowledge
(Greek: *epignosis*)
- Phil. 1:9
- Col. 1:9
- 2 Pet. 1:8

By INCEPTION
(Greek: *gnosis*)
- Rom. 11:33
- 1 Cor. 1:4,5
- Col. 2:1-3

By PERCEPTION
(Greek: *oida*)

K—L

Rom. 8:26,27
13:11
1 Cor. 15:58

LIES—telling lies
(*See also* Truth)

Ps. 119:29
Eph. 4:23-25
Col. 3:9

LIFE

BREVITY of life compared to eternity

Ps. 39:5
102:11,12
James 4:14

The CLEAN life

Job 17:9
Ps. 24:3,4
Is. 52:11

ENJOYING the Christian life

Num. 36:8
Is. 65:22
1 Tim. 6:17

ENJOYING life in general

Eccl. 2:24
3:13
5:18

LIGHT for the believer's journey

Ex. 10:23
Job 22:28
Ps. 119:105,130
Prov. 4:18

L

LIPS of the wise (*See also* Speaking right things with your lips)
> Prov. 10:19
> 12:18
> 15:7
> 16:21,23

LONGEVITY promised by the Lord
> Ex. 23:26
> Job 5:26
> Ps. 91:16
> 92:14
> Is. 46:4

The LORD
ACTS SUDDENLY
> 2 Chron. 29:36
> Mal. 3:1
> Acts 2:2

KNOWS OUR HEARTS
> 2 Chron. 32:31
> Jer. 17:9,10
> Luke 2:35
> Heb. 4:12

WORKS WITHIN US
> Eph. 3:20,21
> Phil. 2:13
> Heb. 13:20,21
> 1 John 4:4

LOVE (*See also* Fruit, Love)
GOD'S LOVE for us
> Jer. 31:3
> Hos. 11:4
> Rom. 5:5

As a DIVINE FORCE
(Greek: *agape*)

L—M

John 15:13
Rom. 5:5
Gal. 5:6

As a HUMAN AFFECTION
(Greek: *phileo*)
John 11:3,36
Titus 3:15

LOWLY—the Lord respects the lowly

Ps. 138:6
Prov. 3:34
11:2
16:19

MIDNIGHT—Actions of the Lord at midnight

Ex. 11:4
Matt. 25:6
Luke 11:5-8
Acts 16:25

MIND

Of the CHRISTIAN
CHRIST'S mind 1 Cor. 2:16
Phil. 2:5
RENEWED Rom. 12:2
SOUND 2 Tim. 1:7
Of the NON-CHRISTIAN
ALIENATED Col. 1:21
BLINDED 2 Cor. 4:3,4
VANITY Eph. 4:17

MIRACLES

Of the APOSTLES

M—N

    Acts 4:16
        8:13
        19:11,12
DIVERSIFIED Heb. 2:3,4
GREAT Acts 8:13 AMP*
Of JESUS John 2:11
                6:2
        Acts 2:22
NOTABLE Acts 4:16
SPECIAL Acts 19:11
For TODAY Job 5:8,9
              John 14:12
              Heb. 2:2-4

MONEY—the futility of money

Is. 55:2
Ezek. 7:19
Zeph. 1:18

NAME of the Lord

Ps. 5:11
    20:7
   113:3
Prov. 18:10
Is. 59:19

NOONDAY—actions of the Lord at noonday

Ps. 55:17
   91:5,6
Song of Sol. 1:7
Acts 22:6

The Amplified Bible, New Testament (La Habra: The Lockman Foundation, 1954, 1958), pp. 185,186.

N—P

NOTHING against us shall prevail
>Ps. 2:12
>27:1-3
>Is. 41:11,12
>54:17
>Rom. 8:31

PEACE (*See also* Fruit, Peace)
Of GOD
>Rom. 15:33
>Phil. 4:7
>Col. 3:15

Of MIND
>Is. 26:3,12
>Phil. 4:7

PROMISED
>Ps. 119:165
>John 14:27
>Phil. 4:7

PLEASURE of the Lord
>Ps. 35:27
>36:8
>149:4

POVERTY—a negative thing for God's people
>Prov. 13:18
>20:13
>23:21
>28:19

POWER
As AUTHORITY (Greek: *exousia*)
>Matt. 10:1
>Luke 10:19
>John 1:12

P

As DOMINION (Greek: *kratos*)
- Eph. 1:19
- 6:10
- Col. 1:10-12

As DYNAMIC power (Greek: *dunamis*)
- Acts 1:8
- 1 Cor. 2:4
- 2 Tim. 1:7

As a STRENGTH AND FORCE (Greek: *ischus*)
- Mark 12:33 (strength)
- 1 Pet. 4:11 (ability)
- Rev. 5:12

PRAISING God's Word

- Ps. 56:4,10
- 119:162
- Jer. 15:16

PRAYER

- Eph. 6:18
- 1 Tim. 2:1
- James 5:16

ANSWERS come
- Ps. 118:5
- 138:3
- Jer. 33:3
- Hab. 2:2

ASKING
- John 14:14
- 15:7,16
- 1 John 3:22
- 5:14,15

INTENSITY needed in prayer
(*See also* Seeking the Lord)
- Ps. 63:8

P

    Jer. 29:13
    Matt. 11:12
  KNOCKING/persistence
    Gen. 32:26
    Matt. 7:7,8
    Luke 18:7,8
  SEEKING
    Ps. 105:4
    Is. 55:6
    Hos. 10:12

PREPARING for the Lord

  2 Chron. 27:6
  Job 11:13-18
  Prov. 24:27

PRIDE—avoiding pride

  Prov. 11:2
      16:18
  Dan. 4:37

PROBLEMS, problems, problems, but the Lord brings us through

  Ps. 34:19
      73:26
  1 Cor. 10:13

PROMISES of God (*See also* Blessings)

  ABSOLUTELY TRUSTWORTHY
    Num. 23:19
    Ps. 89:34
    Ezek. 12:28
  GOD FULFILLS His promises
    Num. 23:19
    Is. 55:10,11
    Ezek. 12:28

P

Luke 1:45

RENEWED STRENGTH (*See also* Strength)

Ps. 84:7
Is. 40:29-31

RETAINING the promises in your memory

Deut. 6:6
Ps. 119:11
Col. 3:16

WILL NOT FAIL

Josh. 21:45
  23:14
1 Kings 8:56

WORK IS COMPLETED

Job 8:7
Ps. 138:8
Rom. 9:28
Phil. 1:6

The YOUNG ARE TAUGHT by God

Ps. 71:17
Eccl. 12:1
Lam. 3:27
1 Tim. 4:12

PROMOTION comes from the Lord

1 Sam. 3:20
Ps. 75:6,7
  147:6
  148:14
Prov. 4:7,8

PROSPERITY—a positive thing for God's people

Josh. 1:8
Job 36:11

P—R

Ps. 35:27

PROTECTION

From ENEMIES
Prov. 16:7
Jer. 1:19
Luke 10:19

For your HOME
Job 11:18,19
Ps. 91:10
Prov. 3:24
24:15

PURITY

GOD'S purity (*See also* Word of God)
James 3:17
Rev. 22:1

SERVING GOD in purity
1 Tim. 5:22
Titus 1:15
1 Pet. 1:22

QUIETNESS

Job 34:29
Eccl. 4:6
Prov. 17:1
Is. 30:15
32:17
2 Thess. 3:12

RELEASE to increase— a paradox

Prov. 11:24,25
Luke 6:38

REQUESTS of the Lord
1 Chron. 4:10
Job 6:8
Phil. 4:6

RESTING
In FAITH
Ex. 33:14
Is. 14:3
Jer. 6:16
Matt. 11:28,29
Heb. 4:9-11

From LIFE'S BATTLES
2 Sam. 7:11
      21:17
Heb. 4:9

RESTORATION
Ps. 23:3
   51:12
Jer. 30:17
Joel 2:25

RETALIATION forbidden
Prov. 24:29
Rom. 12:17
1 Pet. 3:9

REVIVING us
Hos. 6:2

PRAYER for reviving us again
Ps. 85:6
Hab. 3:2

R—S

REWARDS—your efforts rewarded in this life

Ruth 2:12
2 Chron. 15:7
Ps. 58:11

RICHES from the Lord

1 Chron. 29:12
Prov. 10:4
    24:4
Is. 45:3

RIGHTEOUSNESS as clothing for the believer (*See also* Garments)

Job 29:14
Ps. 132:9
Is. 11:5
  59:17
  61:10
Rev. 19:8

RISING and trying again

Ps. 37:24
Prov. 24:16
Jonah 3:1

SAFETY

Deut. 33:12
Prov. 3:23-26
    18:10

SALVATION (*See also* Garments; Joy in salvation)

For your CHILDREN
Is. 49:25
Acts 16:31
Luke 19:9

S

DESCRIPTIONS
- A CUP Ps. 116:13
- A GARMENT Is. 61:10
- A HOPE 1 Thess. 5:8
- A HORN Luke 1:69
- A ROCK Ps. 95:1
- A TOWER 2 Sam. 22:51
- A WELL Is. 12:3

For HUSBAND or wife
- Mal. 3:17
- 1 Cor. 7:12-16
- 2 Pet. 3:9

SATAN

His ACTIVITIES (**Note:** All Christians should refuse to participate in any of Satan's activities.)

ASTROLOGY
- Is. 47:10-13
- Jer. 10:2
- Dan. 1:20

DIVINATION
- Num. 23:23
- Deut. 18:10-12
- Acts 16:16

FAMILIAR SPIRITS—consulting them through astral projection, crystal balls, horoscopes, levitation, Ouija boards, tarot cards, and tea leaf reading
- Lev. 19:31
  - 20:6,27

NECROMANCY—spiritualism, seances involving mediums
- Deut. 18:10-12
- 1 Sam. 28:11
- Is. 8:19,20

S

SORCERY
- Jer. 27:9
- Acts 8:9
- 13:6

WITCHCRAFT
- 1 Sam. 15:23
- 2 Chron. 33:6
- Gal. 5:19-21

ATTEMPTS to ruin men by

APPEARING as an angel of light 2 Cor. 11:14

CUNNING plans and strategies 2 Cor. 2:10,11

LYING promises Gen. 3:4,5

WRESTING the Scriptures Matt. 4:6

His DEFEAT—Jesus defeated Satan for all time at the cross
- John 12:31
- Heb. 2:14
- 1 John 3:8

Our DEFENSE against his works (*See also* Defense)

Bind them in Jesus' name Matt. 18:18-20

Oppose them Eph. 4:27

Resist them James 4:7

The ENEMY of all Christians
- Luke 22:31
- Eph. 6:12
- 1 Pet. 5:8

A FALLEN being
- Is. 14:12
- Luke 10:18
- Rev. 12:9

His POWER
- BROKEN since Calvary Heb. 2:14
- DOOMED Rev. 20:2
- Very LIMITED Job 2:6
- Only PERMITTED Luke 4:6
- RESISTED James 4:7

VICTORY of Christians over Satan is assured
- Ps. 44:5
- 2 Cor. 10:4
- Luke 10:19

WEAPONS we use in winning over him
- BLOOD of Jesus Rev. 12:11
- NAME of Jesus Mark 16:17,18
- PRAISING the Lord 2 Chron. 20:22
- PRAYER James 5:16
- WORD of God Eph. 6:17

His WORKS destroyed by Jesus
- 2 Thess. 2:8
- Heb. 2:14,15
- 1 John 3:8

SEEKING the Lord with all-out intensity
(*See also* Prayer)

Is. 62:6,7
Jer. 29:13
Heb. 11:6
James 5:16

SERVING the Lord (*See also* Anointed by the Holy Spirit for service; Purity)

Ex. 23:25
Acts 20:18,19
    26:6,7

S

    Rom. 12:10,11
EARLY in life and early in the day
    Ps. 63:1
    Prov. 8:17
    Is. 26:9

Our SERVICE well-pleasing to the Lord
    Phil. 4:18
    Col. 3:20
    Heb. 13:16,21

SIGNS and wonders

    Dan. 4:3
    Acts 2:19
         4:29,30
    Heb. 2:3,4

SIN—cleansing from sin

    Ps. 51:2,7
    Is. 1:18
    1 John 1:7

SLEEP (*See also* Body, Sleeplessness)

    Ps. 3:5
        4:8
      127:2
    Prov. 3:24

SONG in the night

    Job 35:10
    Ps. 42:8
    Is. 30:29

S—T

SPEAKING right things with your lips (*See also* Lips of the wise)

> Prov. 12:19
> 22:11
> 23:16

STAND (*See also* Believer—standing firm)

> Hab. 2:1
> Acts 5:20
>
> Stand STILL
>> Ex. 14:13,14
>> Num. 9:8
>> 2 Chron. 20:15,17

STRENGTH for each day (*See also* Renewed Strength)

> Deut. 33:25
> Neh. 8:10
> Is. 27:5
> Zech. 10:12
> Phil. 4:13

SUPPORT from the Lord as we live for Him

> Deut. 33:27
> Is. 41:9,10
> 63:8,9

TEACH ME, Lord

> Ex. 4:12
> Ps. 32:8
> 34:11
> 90:12
> Is. 2:3

T

THINGS

BETTER things—a STUDY IN CONTRASTS
- 1 Sam. 15:22
- Ps. 118:8
- Prov. 15:16,17
- 16:9,16
- Eccl. 6:9

BETTER things TO LOOK FORWARD TO
- Heb. 6:9
- COUNTRY Heb. 11:13-16
- COVENANT Heb. 8:1-6
- HOPE Heb. 7:19
- PROMISES Heb. 8:1-6
- RESURRECTION Heb. 11:35
- TESTAMENT Heb. 7:22

SECRET things of the Lord
- Deut. 29:29
- Ps. 25:14
- Prov. 3:32
- Amos 3:6,7

TIME

As an OPPORTUNITY (Greek: *kairos*)
- Acts 3:19
- Rom. 13:11
- Eph. 5:16

As RECORDED by the clock (Greek: *chronos*)
- Gal. 4:4
- 1 Thess. 5:1
- 1 Pet. 1:17

TREASURES

NEW
- HEART AND SPIRIT Ezek. 36:26

The LORD'S COMPASSIONS
Lam. 3:22,23
THINGS Is. 42:9
OLD
    COUNSELS of old Is. 25:1
    LANDMARK Prov. 23:10
    PATHS Jer. 6:16

TRUSTING in the Lord

Ps. 56:3
    118:8
During TROUBLE (*See also* Deliverance from trouble)
Nah. 1:7

TRUTH—telling the truth
(*See also* Lies)

Prov. 8:7
Zech. 8:16
Eph. 4:15

UNITING affections, intellect, and will

Josh. 24:15
1 Kings 18:21
Ps. 86:11

VICTORY

SHOUTING the victory (*See also* Defeat; Satan, Victory of Christians)
Josh. 6:20
Ps. 47:1,5

VISITATION—divine visitation

Job 7:17,18
    10:12

V—W

Ps. 17:3

WAITING on the Lord

Prov. 20:22
Is. 30:18
   40:31
Lam. 3:25
Mic. 7:7

WATCHING alertly

Matt. 26:41
Mark 13:33
1 Thess. 5:6
1 Pet. 4:7

WAYS of the Lord

Ps. 25:4
Rom. 11:33
Rev. 15:3

WALKING in His ways

Josh. 22:5
1 Kings 2:3
     3:14
      8:57,58
     11:38

WEALTH

FLEETING uncertainty of material wealth

Ps. 62:10
Prov. 27:24
1 Tim. 6:17

WORLD'S wealth transferred to the believer

Job 27:13,16,17
Prov. 13:22
    28:8
Eccl. 2:26

WEAPONS (See Satan, Weapons we use in winning over him)

WIFE—a good wife
Prov. 12:4
  18:22
  19:14
  31:10-12

WINNING others to the Lord
Prov. 11:30
Dan. 12:3
John 4:35
James 5:20

WISDOM

And KNOWLEDGE (understanding)
  Prov. 2:6
  Rom. 11:32
  Col. 2:1-3

ACQUIRING them
  Prov. 4:7
    16:16
    18:15
    19:8

LOCATING them
  Prov. 2:1-5
    3:13
    8:8-11
    8:33-35

A PRECIOUS treasure
  Prov. 24:3,4
  Is. 33:6
  Col. 2:1-3

And POWER—combining them
  Job 12:13 (strength)

W

Matt. 13:54 (mighty works)
1 Cor. 1:23,24

WORD of God

CHOICE words about the Word
Deut. 32:45-47
Ps. 119:133
　147:15
Mic. 2:7
1 Thess. 2:13

God's Word on FIRE
Deut. 4:24
Jer. 5:14
　20:9
　23:29
Luke 24:32

LOGOS—*Logos*, or the Word of God, is all 31,173 verses of the Bible and all the subjects contained therein. It is everything God has left recorded in the Bible for our spiritual instruction—the whole counsel of God. *Logos* is defined as the subject matter, teaching, topic, doctrine, and overview of God's plan for the human race.

Col. 3:16
2 Thess. 3:1
Heb. 4:12

Its PURITY (*See also* Purity, God's purity)
Ps. 12:6
　119:140
Prov. 30:5

RHEMA—*Rhema* is one verse of scripture. It is the confessed word, the creative word,

W

a single promise, utterance, phrase, command, or isolated affirmation. *Logos* is the Bible in its entirety; *rhema* is the Bible by special application. *Logos* is the general word; *rhema*, the specific word.

    John 15:7
    Rom. 10:17
    Eph. 6:17

WORDS

FREE flowing
    Ex. 4:12
    Ps. 81:10
    Prov. 16:1
    Acts 4:31

Your words LIBERATE OR CAPTIVATE
    Job 22:28
    Prov. 18:21
    Matt. 12:37

WORTHY is the Lord to be praised

    2 Sam. 22:4
    Rev. 4:11
        5:9,12

Scriptures on
CONCLUDING MATTERS

Ps. 37:37
Eccl. 7:8
    12:13
Matt. 24:13

Dick Mills is intensely involved in the Scriptural renewal and personal upbuilding of the Body of Christ. He shares the "hidden riches of secret places" with sensitivity and compassion. Few have failed to be touched by the hand of God through this man's dynamic ministry.

Pat Robertson, president of Christian Broadcasting Network, says: "Dick Mills has one of the most unique ministries of any man of God I know. God has gifted him with what amounts to a photographic memory containing thousands of scriptures. Under the anointing of the Holy Spirit and at an appropriate time, these words are brought forth to minister to the needs of individuals. Dick has been used of God to bring deep spiritual blessings at crucial times in my own life, and I'm sure this is true of tens of thousands of others around the country."

Dick and his wife Betty live in Hemet, California. This veteran of over thirty years has ministered to more than twenty denominations in countries throughout the world, including Israel, England, Australia, Singapore, Canada, and Latin America.

Write: Dick Mills • P. O. Box 758 • Hemet, CA 92343

For additional copies of this book, write:
Harrison House • P. O. Box 35035 • Tulsa, OK 74153